Dark Poems of Elsewhere

by Bob Stevens

ISBN 13: 979-8-9852929-0-9

Printed in the United States of America

First Printing: 2021

25 24 23 22 21   5 4 3 2 1

jrefund no. 3 (2021)

Other Books by Bob Stevens

Dark Tales of the Inland Seas Region

Dark Poems of the Inland Seas Region

Dark Poems of Elsewhere

by Bob Stevens

Table of Contents

the fallen angel bar and grill

last night that old goatee devil

was pacing the frozen skid walk outside his club

dangerous pink silk shirt

open like a flower

red chested and glistening hot

flesh steam on the rise

snow, with gentle drifting descent

on the fall

there was a definite air of nervousness in his
motions

a twitch of worried thought arched one eyebrow

with a quick and angry thumb

he flicked the ash off his cigarette

it drifted with a silent crash

to the garbage-strewn pavement

the devil gave a hairy scratch to his adam's apple

and the movement dislodged

some leaves of cash from his frame

to the ice and he thought

well, fuck it

my damn pockets are stuffed

the cash registers inside are all stuffed

without a doubt

and as if that isn't quite enough, well, friend

the waitstaff and bartenders

have fishbowls full of generous tips

it keeps pilin' up when you have

the best show in town

the fallen angel bar and grill

as anyone could see

was on fire and in full swing

rafter packed with more sinners en route

parking cockeyed at curbside blocks away

and away and away

another big friday night gained momentum

the devil yawned

then the devil paused

boredom and concern jousted in his brain

quite disquieting opponents

his red lips tingled with memories

of a true love's kiss

while sucking a white cigarette

it was then he noticed

a patrol car, one he'd seen before

inching down the yellowy streetlight avenue

engine purr, crunch of snow, sirens ominously
silent

the only sound was the muffled

thump and blare of the band inside

saxophone trombone trumpet clarinet accordion
violin

the chunk and slap of an upright bass

the devil's music

the boys in blue rolled up

passenger side window gliding down

good evening

said a voice familiar with words like

apprehend and perpetrator and premises and
violation

good evening, sir, it said, everything alright
tonight

the devil took a few bills from his ass pocket

placed them with long fingers into the officer's
oily palm

yes, everything is fine, you know, officer sir

drugs live sex torture booze and underage and
murder

he chuckled

the cop, that is

and put the money in the glovebox without
counting it

then he just looked at the devil

kinda sizing up his suit

the officers silent smirking appraisal lingered

and satan, impatient

unzipped and took his long dangle cock out

you can suck this or leave, he said

the cops left

the devil yawned again

and went back inside

using long jerky strides

through the heavy vine-covered crypt style club
doors

and into a wall of noise and smoky red light

torch fires burning and acrid drugs burning

the air was full of grave fiends

in swooping flight

like bats beneath

the high cathedral domed ceiling

their mighty rubbery black wings

billowing the smoke to clear

they dipped and twirled

and tore chunks out of one another

with razor teeth and reaching talons

tiny blood splashes on the heads of the wicked
below

and near the bandstand

demonic strippers in black iron cages

threw knives into the crowd

and the crowd was thick

the old devil navigated the oversexed throng

with distracted, annoyed steps

very much like his outside cloven pacing

he couldn't find his wife anywhere

didn't matter at the moment

she was around

he could feel her proximity fluttering

like a bloody moth trapped

in his red lightbulb heart

sweet lilith, sweet deadly night blossom, my
love

his heart ached, to be alone again with you

my everything

she was around

up to no good

probably covered in blood

and flashing her fangs on the dancefloor

snapping necks at random for more bodies to
boil

more skeletons to extract

for the bone rooms in the basement

the devil opened his stench hole mouth

and felt his heart crack as he yawned

concern was dealing boredom

some heavy damage

then, as he pushed his way roughly through the
bodies

his eyes were drawn to a change

a large live oak tree had grown huge by the
bandstand

it looked like

louisiana

and the band wailed appropriate dixie slop

a man with a bottle navigated the mangle of
branches

as the patrons went convulsive with excitement

this man was wearing a shabby suit, a dusty black fedora

and, much more thrilling

he was wearing a noose

he shimmied along a branch

over the hot kettle of the crowd

and looked down with glassy wide eyes of self-destruction

like a madman above the storm

windswept and drenched

his wooden coffin already complete somewhere

he tied his rope tightly and glared at the creatures below

with that familiar dead-end gaze

that trumpeted the sentiment

yes, fuck you all, i wish the whole rotten human

race

had one single neck and my strangle hands were
on it

(mercy, mercy)

he made a sweeping vulgar gesture

laughed an asylum laugh

and then, as anticipated

jumped to his quick

neck crack

of a death

the body swung in a creaking heave from side to
side

like a lantern on a stormy ship and

piss leaked in a glistening line

from his pant leg as he twirled

and a man wearing a red feather boa and

nothing else

caught it in his wine glass and called bottoms up

the devil stretched and yawned

a small orgy

involving some hodgepodge of sailors

started

at the base of the tree and then

from the rafters came the crows

screeching and flapping and

well

carrion is carrion

oh boredom

oh worry

where is my lovely wife, the devil groaned

panic, desperation and melancholy teamed up

to produce a single tear

that rolled slow down his cheek

and he yawned and yawned

and yawned

she's probably in jail

and our lady refused the doctors

our lady from blue to black to white

was a sight to behold

sometimes prim and proper with a rose

pinned to her dress

changing from bloody red to blue

when she danced cheek to cheek

to shuffling weepy songs played on the stereo

she was our lady of the blue hours in that bar

and how she wore the color of blue

the color of blue became her

she wore that blue-jeweled second-hand
necklace

our lady of the bombay sapphire

blue juniper berry spell

our lady of the still flexible but fallen

legion of blue ballerinas

and the progression of her hours moved

toward the blue of endtime

the moon white and blue of bones

the slutty blue of cleopatra mascara

all watery and sinister these frozen hues, these
blues

and the blue of nevermore was so similar in
shade

to the moods of our lady

because she was our lady

of both the coughing and the deep sighs

and our collective adoration lifted her

to hover holy above us

often you'd find her pounding the piano

the one stuck behind the pool tables

hard and angry as if punishing the keys

for old sad tunes played

her hair so tempting for birds to nest in

and the snow whipping by the bar window

the city all twinkles of electric velveteen

a lapping wave of the edison shimmers

her little piano tears

turning the view of the street outside to stars

screams raining down from the upper floors

crashing through the vents like gas fire

then with her hands up she would sing

my fingers are clean of rings

men just don't marry such women, they don't, la
la

but will it concern me whatsoever

no, in fact, it won't

it would be suicide with moonflowers and
vaudeville

it would be worthless and old-fashioned and ill-
advised

i could call her medusa because of my burden

but i call her our lady of the blackstems instead

and how she wore the color of black

the color of black became her

our lady of the self-inflicted black bruises

and black scowling moods

our lady of the elongated eye teeth and black
cape

the black of dried blood around stiletto cut
wounds

our lady svengali of the lightless bottom

beneath the sliding black river

where murdered corpses

ankled in concrete

quiver their rotting shoulders

with the bubbling jabs and pokes

of the black fishes feeding

sunken murders with eye sockets

black as the black of our lady

our somber lady of the midnight mistakes

all of which were so easy to make

swept up in the great oblivion

of that perpetual shadow-trap of closing time

that drinking hole where the sun is only seen

in photographs and rarely missed

our lady of the night owls

and our lady of hopeless causes

she could steal your careless heart

and keep it from you, a hostage

sometimes for a weekend or a month

then she'd return it

still beating but broken

declaring it her ambition to spend the rest of her
hours

unattached and dreaming

and wedding vows be damned

asleep or awake the reverie of this floating life

must continue

she'd say

i suppose now that you know this

you are anxious to hear a detailed description

of this oddball who vexed

so many homesick strangers

well, seek out a blurry photo

of theda bara unbearably vampish

then imagine her at the end of a bender

that was our lady

our lady of the diminishing charms

she could turn so monstrous

when drinking with weapons at hand

she never wanted to discuss the stories behind
her scars

the white scars like chalk marks on a sun-
blanched tomb

and how she wore the color of white

the color of white became her

our martyred lady

of the ripped white stockings

our lady of heaven's peerless brothel

adorned with misplaced white glowing nimbus

our lady of the white rats

which infested the hull of the ship

that brought her here

hopping off at nightfall

all dressed in white

our lady swam to the lower east side

which is where she lit her little white cigarettes

for the rest of her days

she was our lady of the white powders

and the all-nighters

the white of the sheets

and the whites of her eyes rolled back

the white of the bathroom tiles

where she was found with white foam on her
chin

then the white of the unavoidable

tomb and shroud and headstone

all of which obsessed her

she was from some far-off

snowbound land of phantoms

or so her fantastic brand

of embellishments did claim

but from wherever

our lady of the letdowns hailed

she had dragged her homeland ghosts

along with her

she wore their possessive threadbare ranks

like a cape

you could see them billowing behind her

as she fixed her lipstick

in a dusty compact mirror

all unfastened and unfurled

like a yawning clam shell

our lady of the ghastly pallor was known to
many

as simply unreachable

she languished along half crazed

and carried with her an air of the forbidden

her powdery sickbed complexion

(made more deathly by booze)

could cast strange and incurable spells

but now

the snow falls and the moon

has lost sight of what happened to her

none of us can tell between drinks

and all of us are to blame

but from blue to black to white

it happened so fast

and now our lady our love

and our occasional hope

is gone

she's still waiting for that asshole

she is out there

soaked to the bone

long hair of black yarn framing

the smudged porcelain of her face

like a rag doll recovered from a marsh

sad carolina rose

dreaming in the prickly confines

of a growing nest of last straws

a fool if there ever was one

surrounded by

the lush green roll of low country

that catches the shrill downpour

to sparkle with silver beads

on kudzu and lily pads

thunderstorm booming

a volley of car alarms

water frogs begin to tune up

in the messy chamber of the marshes

and the tree frogs start their lewd
communications

unseen in the rockabye branches above

frogs everywhere

but the ribbet and gargle stops

when she walks by

ripples of silence

spreading a wake

for her sleepless wandering

along the road and over the bridge

she moves out into the chattering night

of tall pine

swampy clouds of insects under a gas station
oasis

glowing, one light failing in staccato

lightning strikers of blue spark crackle

and then the clouds break up

to expose a sun rolling off to burn a day
elsewhere

leaving vapor trails of exhaust

from its angry red-hot engine

then snakes emerge from the tall grass

glistening as if just born

others loop like lengths of rope

from the sturdy oaks

as the sun falls

she misses

his picaresque hands

on the pool hall gravel rooftop

the old pool hall that burned down two years
ago

leaving nothing but an open space

where her memory continues to work like a
painter

etching out the boundaries and the old colors
once again

the resurrection of an image

from that trash heap of recollections bronzed

the way he used to grip his belt buckle

and rock on his knees

the way he used to spit

at the mention of church

how he made those wrinkles in his forehead

when wisecracking

and the way he could open beer bottles

with that yellow snarl

and roll a cigarette

with one hand

always pausing

to hold it aloft when finished

as if expecting applause

she misses him

she misses the tinhorn manner he had

of parading her into the bar

and the way he used to sing

in the shower

she sees him in the flesh

on conjugal visits

and she sees him in spirit

every goddamn place she goes

then a car rolls by flying

the bitch and moan war flag

of country music

over the bridge that rust flakes a shower

to ripple the water below

new characters moving out into the tropical soak

while she counts the days

until his parole hearing

and watches another summer go by

friday night call to arms

there is always a safer option

some nobler drift of sober grace

there are methods and religions

to keep the passions in their place

there is always the one that got away

i could mope and think of her

brood my way along silently

but i'd much rather prefer

blowing a big red party horn

on this black death train

it's a locomotive rocking southbound rails

all steam and thunder and pops

you can hear the racket of depravity

and this racket never stops

hanging out of a window i can see

a lady with no clothes

she's holding on for dear life

getting fucked on tippy toes

i can hear a big red party horn

on this black death train

those aboard all have a taste for thrills

and with a healthy swallow of brine

they're extracting the spirit from the flesh

all up and down the line

of course the express is never stationary

but to call it progress would be wrong

just a stunning deception of movement

that can be yours for a song

played on a big red party horn

on this black death train

so for the passionate and reckless

for the impatient and unglued

for all the confetti and flying corks

for those sick of feeling blue

and for those who won't go quietly

for the mambo, twist and bone

for marking the end with crazy friends

instead of dying all alone

let's blow a big red party horn

on this black death train

to the last station past oblivion

where a conga line of happy knaves

departs all weaving and wasted

into a field of open graves

they've left behind some crazy stories

and their car keys and their cares

making room for passengers like me

who board regardless of bewares

to blow a big red party horn

on this black death train

let's blow a big red party horn

on this black death train

stay away from the waitstaff

the far-off sway

of the low lady moon

a tropical bead of blue

above the waves

trapped by gravity

stuck in orbit for all to see

a prisoner held aloft

in the open flue

of eventide

the low lady moon

that was charlie's focus

he stood outside listening to the ocean

looking up over the palm trees

saw the moon throb and shiver

felt his body turn gravy

melted and melting gravy

charlie was viciously inebriated

launched in a morpheus updraft

and way too high to be in public

too high to function

way way too high

and now, he lamented

and now i am engaged in a hopeless battle

to maintain some respectable facade

some thespian sobriety

oh, impossible task

he asked that pretty low lady moon for help

but she slipped behind a cloud

vanishing with a little wink as if to say

you and all the other solitary wrecks

of this balmy evening

are unfortunately on your own

i have lovers to shine on

so farewell

charlie traced his steps back

how did he get like this

it wasn't the seven beers at the bar

and it wasn't the occasional nip

from his flask of rum

this certainly wasn't the familiar

loopy buzz of alcohol

it was those ten minutes

on the side of the restaurant

lighting up with two mangy members of the
waitstaff

that's when his buzz

became a jet engine roar of numb floating

whatever he smoked with those local boys

was heavy and probably laced

he made a fist

next time i see those fucking waiters

then he stopped

realizing two things

one

he was talking out loud

and two

a crowd had gathered

44

dinner guests

evening attire

sequins

the hilarity of tuxedoes

these fancy pants had gathered to listen

they had gathered to watch him sway

not so furtively pointing

finding amusement

in the poor leaning tower

of charlie

whose general motion adhered to

the rhythm of the waves

his knees bending slightly

with each new

beach crash

with each new

beach crash

with each new

they wouldn't laugh if they knew

how hard this is, he thought angrily

time to rid myself of these corny fucks

so he turned toward them

and smiled

a smile that had been weaponized

by bad life choices

miscolored and broken and missing

this smile took their breath away

caused them to step back

the familiar flinching choreography

of a communal gasp

a collective withdrawal

he kept smiling

until every last face had turned away

moments later

the band in the next room broke the tension

with the blare of horns and some hypnotic
percussion

rolling beats that softened the crowd

and moved bodies in close

a romantic tune

the weaving melody

picked up the pace to a hipshake

and our boy tumbled into the crowd

bouncing from one body to the next

some of those irritated with his lack of
coordination

shoved him in the back as he passed

and planted kicks to the calf

with sharp dress shoes

it was hard enough to walk already

but he made it through

found a wall

there he leaned himself

legs aching

and tried to regain some composure

slicking his hair back with both hands

working his way into a contemplative stare

instead he kept licking his lips

it wasn't working

he was too thirsty

but fighting the crowd to the bar

seemed a grim prospect

he'd have a cigarette and think on the matter

there were only four left in the pack

he managed to get one on his lips

when a bright flash in front of his eyes

initially mistaken for a distant explosion

hopefully in the kitchen

(fucking waiters)

turned out to be a woman with a lighter

finally some class and thank you he said

after he leaned into the flame

and was on his way

she remained, expressionless

bulging out of a black gown

blonde hair pinned up

dreadful orange skin

he nodded at her again

thanks

really

now scram

she looked a while longer

shaking her head

and then turned to leave

the band was playing a new song

the stage lights

had gone from red to shadow

obscuring the musicians

but you could tell

they were all slowly moving

for a moment or two

charlie felt completely relaxed

not a care in the world

the percussionist stood in front of a tribal
marimba

made with skulls in a variety of species and sizes

and he conked out

a creeping

lurching

rhythm

taking his cue

a domestic long hair with a violin

stepped forward

into a new hot circle of stage light

and bent his bow to rend a heartbreaking note

then a cornet

joined by more muted brass

providing a new lush carpet of sound for the
violinist

who played more of his terrible sweaty lament

charlie looked down

and noticed he was missing his left shoe

even worse, his big toe poked through a sock
hole

christ, he said to himself

fucking embarrassing

a man approached him

slicked down proper

and in a lovely low country brogue

reached out and said

you are right

this is fucking embarrassing

but you have the option

to leave this place with some dignity

with me as your very temporary escort

shall we

he gently flapped an invitation

with his rooster arm

but something about the motion

resulted in immediate

and overpowering

nausea

his throat burned

he lurched up and

out it spewed

on sleeves and slacks and shoes

charlie managed a gurgled half-apology

before heaving once more

now he'd done it

he was going to get kicked out

again

sure enough

the next set of hands on his body

belonged to a large and very strong bouncer

charlie was hoisted up and carried off

feet dragging on the floor

he looked apologetically into the faces he passed

but this only seemed to inspire more horror

he saw one woman faint

then he was on some kind of porch

and when the bouncer's arms withdrew

he collapsed as if shot by several bullets at once

straight to the ground

where he settled

eyes closed

head spinning

he decided

to just lay there

awhile

consoling himself by remembering

a curious natural phenomenon

a volcanic area in africa

where carbon monoxide leaks in a mist

over a grassy green paradise garden

littered with bones and carcasses

they say all who enter

unless the wind is right

succumb almost instantly

predators collapsing on prey

freed from struggle

and at peace with enemies

he formed this picture in his mind

and floated away

the lovely consuelo kisses the old matador

in the lobby was a bull's head

with a wreath tiara of brittle roses

dusty webbed silky

over a flowerpot of dead dry ivy

the man behind the counter

was listening to pedro infante

fizzled with radio static

the romantic sentiments struggled to be heard

the bulls head spit out a cockroach

that vanished like a spill

into the gashlike shadow beneath its bristle chin

consuelo and the old matador were having a
moment

initially by torment

then by the following grace of quieter years

the tornado of living had dropped them

into the same warm evening

and they stood there like old movie stars

beneath the crackling strobe of a florescent light

her curve hugging red dress

on fire

each movement a spray of sizzling brilliance

her big belly and big belly-dancer hips

waves of brunette shot with silver

falling over almond shoulders

both their faces wrinkled

from decades of squinting and grudges

he whispered about his career

he couldn't help himself

his career of sweeping flamenco moves

in a one ring circus with sixty other clowns

sixty other clowns who tore his little heart out

all stitched together like some musty rag doll

they ripped it from his breast

buried it in the sawdust there

while the orchestra played a funeral march

and the bleachers rocked with laughter

gored in the sands

of a hot sun bloodbath

far away from this carolina

in old mexico

she said hush

be quiet

i know

louise and the ocean that carries her

midnight is approaching

and the ocean skies

release a thousand shivers of rain

gusted shimmering night curtains

draped from the somber heavens down

into the white-tipped furious waves

sizzling there on the foaming summits

and the sad groaning of a passenger ship

can be heard as it holds to its course

iron rivets creaking in their welded construction

responding to each lurching rise

and plunging fall

rhythmic orchestration

for the red-breasted turmoil

that rages in a freshly wounded heart

a freshly wounded heart that resides

glowing like a firelit ruby inside a woman

aboard that ship

hidden in one of the cabins

it is louise who has left me

louise the bulgarian beauty

who loved vodka and marine biology

has gone transatlantic

peering through a hissing window

into the slashing confusion of the storm

in her mind there is an image

held there like a ghost above a seance

it's of me and her heart swells

it's of me and she misses me

she must

i wish her safe passage

but there is so much to consider

out in the briny deep

from the east pacific rise

to the mariana trench

to pearlfish and tangleweed

and blowfish and the massive horny cockfish

batfish and bloodfish leaving dark clouds

to obscure the pretty damselfish

and a velvet swimming crab scurries

with closing time eyes into a rocky hole

while up there above

the devil rays and requiem sharks glide by

flying beneath seagrass meadow skies

in dappled blue light

a monstrous squid tightens its grip

on a russian submarine she has brought down

suction cup legs retracting possessively

beak mouth snapping open and shut

squawking bewares and back offs

this is mine

and low in the groaning

kelp curtains of the seabed

lies a scarlet treasure chest

dressed in rusty chains

padlocked and rocking

under the gentle confused touch

of the soupy tide

filled with pistols and coins

guarded by two skeletons

draped with the black hula sway

of oily seagrowth

one in a swashbuckling hat

the other in a gray-jeweled turban

they play bubble spewing accordions

when they sense the unseen moon

grow full in the lost airy world above

and the songs they choose range in subject
matter

from waltzes about savannah

to polkas for portuguese women

always songs about women eventually

forsaken women these sailors relinquished to
ride

away from shore all bravado

straight into a capsized big sleep

their bravery for leaving love

has been rewarded with this undying vigil

over useless treasure

lamentable spirits whose winsome melodies rise

notes trapped in bubbles ascending in order

upwards they break the heaving surface

to follow the seamless horizon like smoke

a moving fogbank of longing and sorrow

prompting a nautical crying

from the whales who groan in sonar

their once carefree gliding migration

now grief-stricken and diverted

by the song of the dead sailors

it drives the sensitive giants suicidal

so they decorate the sea with whines

and great flapping clouds of gore

as they ram into the slicing briar of the reef

and need i remind you

louise is out there as well

and in her mind is an image

an image of me

and her heart swells

an image of me

and she misses me like crazy

seasick green she groans

heartsick blue she knows

she never in a million years

should've left this boy behind

and elsewhere in the ocean that carries her

there is a bevy of well-hipped mermaids

and they lounge about

looking into cloudy vanity mirrors

checking the placement of fiery sea flowers

in the rising and moving clouds of their hair

they purse their kissy red lips

pout at the red-faced sailors

then sink back into the waves laughing

sliding their sleek bodies against one another

wrapping tails and spinning

a downward ballerina spiral

and sometimes

they piss each other off

and fight

vicious but rarely fatal

the loser eventually retreating

into some gloom of deeper waters

to sulk awhile so blue

poor mistreated weeping she-creature

but they always return

to their communal lounging eventually

in time to get dolled up

for whatever ship rolls by next

and yes, they love the rocking waves

and yes, they love the paddling soar of fast
swimming

and true they love everything so much it's
problematic

and not far from those mythical lovelies

just over a ridge

and a reef

then several fathoms down

there's the jagged silhouette of a sunken castle

half crumbled and clustered with anemone and
shells

an interior chamber decorated by white sand

all that remains of the unburied bones

of lost royalty

there is hardly any light

and if bats could live underwater

this is where you'd find them roosting

but roosting instead are lumps

of dimly glowing barnacles

strange rooms to wander through

when you consider

that the last king and queen

had openly screwed here once

notoriously and almost constantly

and even while their castle sank

so the story goes

now sand rises a little each year

rippled and in dunes and growing

the once lavish chambers now languish

and the whole castle hangs

with a blue deep-water silence

so haunted and sad and plagued with memories

creaking and falling down in the steady
progression

of disintegration and washaway

and burial by the weight of a tide that never

ceases

a tide that outlives us all and keeps working

the same unfeeling tide that pulls

too many ships

too far away

and somewhere

on a steamer

my louise, my soul

calls my name out desperately

backhand to forehead

in fits of sleepless longing

she must

he took her with a sigh

late june by luna

a sickle edged to blacken the shade

cows sleeping draped in moss

the earth a mess of puddles from the storm

gone now to spark the horizon over the ocean

made eerie by the remnants of oak, crumbling

around the house that cradled a death of hearts

shrinking to bones

blackened like paper smoldered down

the town and the husband both sleeping

she crept out to the porch swing

sway and squeak the dripping leaves

as the stranger arrived

by chevrolet and twilight

the poetry that came from his kiss-hungry lips

distracted her eyes from his prison tattoos

her eyes, the last living part of her,

were enough to finish the charm

and then

the weave of the wick sparked

as if underwater, barely audible

then three things happened

the porch swing squeaked empty

the crepe myrtle galaxied purple blooms

and the stranger took her with a sigh

song of the three sisters

and the three sisters were singing

in the moments before their murder

a song about the many distempers

and disasters of the heart

when their killers came

armed with bibles and knives

angry and vicious

with boot kicks to the door

pouring in and applauded by

the crystal shatter of glass

their killers came on through

an owl watching from a nearby tree

an owl who heard the three sisters singing

apparently resigned to their execution

they were singing come find us

they were singing come find us again

then the red wave swept over them

what a frothy storm

alcohol fumes and scarlet hands

sister heads yanked back by long hair

three figures in white nightgowns

dragged outside

each thumped by knives

and singing defiantly

three sisters unwed

had their spinster bodies and skirts

reduced to cruel gashes and flaps

a mess of gore given to the swamp

bound by ankle chains and weighed down

with a rusty ship anchor

their gore blessed the leech beds

beneath still water

water that deepened

with the tide from the creeks

and when the men left in their trucks

to drink beer in the satanic light of a bonfire

stoked to turn their bloody overalls to smoke

the night birds quietly called

back and forth

a song about the many distempers

and disasters of the heart

in perfect harmony

on that first night

and on many nights that followed

the dead sisters were singing

come find us again

climbing in a mist

and rising from swamp water

the killers could see them

more and more often

in the trees sometimes

identical black scab gashes

unzipped below their chins

long thick corkscrews of hair on each head

infested sashes framing

three cadaver faces

the moonglow unable to replenish

their old envious sunshine blonde

they had been beautiful

these three sisters

now not so much

now crooked and thin

now malnourished

by the monstrous inability to rest

their milky eyes exposed in black shell sockets

like wet pearls

and they were singing

a song that was just a breeze to the innocent

but to the guilty a growing burden

they sang

the sun gives up on the world

for half the hours on the clock

and that's when reason

can be dashed upon the rocks

allowing the lovely and the profane

to flourish anew

the sisters were singing come find us

and they sang sometimes

kindred spirits never locate one another

in darklands where miracles are rare

and sometimes they find one another and flee

stripping the rose gardens bare

the hand of love leaves many untouched

and the many untouched persist

just listen

and look

up there

they settle on their oak tree perch

in those big branches

six dangling decomposed legs

the binding chain looped a mossy garland

from bony ankle to bony ankle

three sisters

the first alert and watching

with a nose rotted to black apple seeds

her claw hands flaking bits of wet bark away

she would lead the song

and her siblings would follow

the second cradling in her arms

a fragile stillborn babe

all wrapped and silent

she rocked the tiny skeleton

and wept her contribution

pulling beetles from the babe's dry mouth

her touch sapping them of life

they dropped

like berries for the lizards and snakes below

and the third sister had been slaughtered last

hands cut off

the cave of her mouth howled

a speechless breeze that gave an angry shake

to the leaves

causing night birds to fly away

carrying the song of the sisters

to the porches of the guilty

carrying chills as easily as twigs

building darker nesting places now

in the hearts of the guilty

in the hearts of the dying

in the hearts of the dead

how walter truth lost his derby

last night in the dim misty air out there

in the crags and rolls of the foothills

east of the mountains

down a long-suffering trail

of wagon tracks and horseshoe divets

came a lonesome bent-backed traveler

his name was walter truth

he wore a derby and

his horse was in bad shape

a bony gray nag

with a palsy shake

of age and exhaustion

in better days a beauty

proud was his trot, chin held high in georgia

sunshine

but now a wreck of an animal, an aching shell

from all the around and up and down the rough
roads

they'd been traveling for over three months now

through filthy towns and dirt

and clay and eventually mountain trails

going north

now nightfall

a distant heavy purr of thunder

it was sure to be a rainy night

walter shifted his weight in the saddle

and let his mind wander back a few hours

the clip clop duo had pulled into

a small mountain town at dawn

and the day

at its golden offset

felt new and lucky

this will be the day that old mr. truth strikes
gold again

he decreed, but it didn't work out that way

what was his occupation, well

walter truth was either

a run-of-the-mill traveling salesman

or a low life scum-sucking con artist

depending on how you looked at it

he liked to think that he delivered

soothing moments of hope into people's
otherwise

drear and dismal lives

his products, after all, promised happiness

and although they didn't deliver

he saw that promise

as what he was truly selling

and well worth the price

still, each town he sold well in

became a town dangerous to return to

the routine would run as follows

he would set up in a downtown area

right on the street

to proudly display the contents of his saddlebag

always taking his time

with the actual set up to attract attention

and once a crowd gathered

he'd clear his throat and begin

using his most regal and respectable dulcet
delivery

you, beautiful lady, there in the blue

why worry about wrinkles any longer, beautiful
lady

why

i have just the thing for you

right here, ah yes, the blue bottle

see how it shines when i hold it up to the light

all the way from the exotic east

acquired on one of my numerous trips by
pachyderm

distilled with equator spring water

yes, it's true

and secret powders

the west may never understand

we all must answer to the hourglass eventually

but my lady

lovely lovely lady

there is no longer any need to shrivel and dry
out

growing old no longer means looking old

please, step right up

hold it in your hands

feel its warmth radiate

undiluted magic and for such a small price

the inscription on the blue bottle

in rigid block letters

said restore skin and restore youth

now that was quite appealing

to men and women alike

but mr. truth also had lotions

that he had specially designed for the menfolk

guaranteed to increase

strength and muscles and virility

why get pushed around by street bullies any
longer

mr. truth would trumpet

his fist shaking revolution in the air

rub this on before sleep and within a week

mark my words

you'll be pushin' back

and knockin' heads

and chippin' teeth

yes, it's true, my word is golden, remember my
name

walter truth is known from the coast of maine

to the white beaches on the gulf of mexico

come forward, see for yourself

touch

taste

see the indications on the label

restore muscles, grow muscles

restore and grow muscles

and for such a small price

his pitch, back when he and the horse first
started out

had made him a fair amount of money

but the further north into the mountains he
ventured

the worse things had become

he hadn't made a single sale in days

not one

even the horse knew things were bad

and if he could've squeezed his horsy heart

to a permanent standstill

he surely would've done it last night

like a curse

it had all been getting worse

the roads, their luck, everything

now advancing clouds took his moon away

and winter was closing in

autumn had arrived

a few early dry red leaves

already brightened the trail

where walter truth and his horse

counted the bends

and the nights, once fallen

could now produce a teeth chatter and a shiver

soon a diamond glisten of frost by dawn

very soon

worst of all

they were lost

the last town far behind, no new town in sight

and the thunderclaps were no longer a distant
purr

they were blasting off overhead like wartime
cannons

lightning sent jagged and quick columns

of blue light through the branches

and the branches flipped and twirled

and shook under sway

of an eastern bound stiff wind

thick with moisture

but still no rain fell

so walter slapped the reins

whistled through gap teeth

let's go, let's go

and they rode onward

perhaps it was the combined stress

of nasty weather

and empty pocket

but it wasn't long

before mr. truth felt his pain return

a sharp pain in his lower back

like rusty forks in his flesh

jesus and the saints give me strength, he called out

and then reached into

one of his brown leather saddlebags

first grabbing his white label whiskey by the neck

and then

after fishing around for a few teeth-clenched
moments

he came up with a skinny medicine bottle

the label was stained and bore the picture of an
angel

arms outstretched, oh peaceful visage

the angel of mercy

under the black cap inside the bottle

praise the lord

were morphine pills

mr. truth shoveled a few into his mouth

with splotchy fat hands

probably a few too many

but lately the pains had been arriving more
frequently

and he'd been building up a tolerance for the
drug

hafta see a doctor in the next town

he reminded himself

my meager supply is runnin' low

he washed the pills down

with a shot of that whiskey

grinning all wrinkle faced

lips pressed together

as he put both bottles away carefully

walter straightened his posture

already feeling a little better

shelter now, he said quietly to himself

we must find shelter

the trees started a furious shake of flying leaves

and the rain

a temper tantrum frenzy of rain

finally unleashed

fell torrential fast

and clamorous thick

gales blowing ocean strong

the thunder louder and louder

as the horse splashed blindly through the slip of
mud

mr. truth imagined drunk angels

on a drifting storm cloud

creating the thunder by taking turns

rumbling sticks on a massive brass kettle drum

flapping their wings

and kicking empty wine bottles

probably should've stayed in that town

whatever it was called

walter thought

but that place was no good for the likes of me

so onward in the muddy dirge

onward

by ragged road, by tangled woodland

by the noisy black river and the shadow roar of
the forest

by frightened saucer eyes in the underbrush

by thunder and rain and treeshake

and lightning bolt and minute

by minute

by morphine

bye bye

walter carelessly let his hand drift from his

derby

and off it flew

like a bird released from a longtime cage

dammit, he spit, the sharp rain pelting his face

hold it, horsey

i do declare

i lost my goddamn derby

in the pound and splash he dismounted

the dripping nag was obedient and waited

head down

creaking back and forth on brittle knobby knees

trying hard not to notice

the red slits of wolf eyes in the trees

while walter chased after his hat

he slipped and fell once

sliding across the mud on his rear

the morphine

was working now

once on his back

with the dark rain collapsing

he felt a dream

coming on like rolls of

liquid carpet unfurled, muslin and

soft and perfumed came this

dream

a wondrous dream of

beautiful maidens

splashing

yes, splashing in pools of money

while walter

in a three piece

greenback suit and golden string tie

smoked a foot-long cigar

blowing smoky dollar signs

like clouds to the moon

the high moon

oh, a truly wondrous dream there in the mud

he wasn't exactly sure

if he ever wanted to rise again

then a bright flash of lighting

a mountain quake of thunder

and he saw his derby getting away

it wheeled on its side

and lifted on the wind

carrying over the roadside weeds

and into the shaking woods

walter scrambled to his pin cushion feet and
followed

oh, what a beautiful nightmare

he said as he trudged on

eyes throwin' off sparks

under the canopy of trees

he could see a bit better

once his eyes had adjusted

and he wiped the wetness away

there he found his precious derby

propped against a tree trunk

thank you, jesus

a man ain't nothin' without a good hat

he snagged it

fixed it tightly on his round buzzing head

and then

his peripheral vision caught something

a light

off through the rainy forest was an orange light

a tiny boxlight

a window frame through the downpour

he let out a whoop and a holler

a house in the woods

a house

warm and dry and maybe

with a potential customer inside

he hurried back to the road

fetched his exhausted horse

and the clip clop duo

quickly made their way through black tangles

a bolt of lightning split a tree with a shower of
blue sparks

and woodchips and then a creaking timber crack
and fall

walter and horse were almost crushed to death

shit and more shit, he cursed

come on, horsey

rain

rain

rain

and then they made

the porch of the tiny house

walter roped the horse to the poorly cut wooden
rail there

and turned to look at the mountain shack

the two-bit cabin

what a goddamn dump, he thought

but it'll hafta do

he rubbed his hands together

alright, time to turn on the charm

and when he knocked loudly

the door fell open

he removed his derby

poked his head inside

hello

anybody here

it was a poor man's two-room cabin

one sittin' room

and one sleepin' room, well

no one was in the sittin' room

but a fire was burnin' high

a fireplace red and orange blaze

no one around

good

walter grabbed his saddlebag of potions and
lotion

and turned to his horse

sit tight, i'm goin' in

he slipped through the door

quietly shutting it behind him

his intentions, upon finding the place empty,
had changed

morphine loopy eyes scanned the firelit room

looking for something to steal

figuring that the owner was

probably some old geezer either lost in the rain

or asleep in the back room full of corn liquor and

hell, there might even be money in here, who
knows

he set his drip drop saddlebag

with a soft clink to the floor

and tiptoed in

holding his breath with each floorboard crack

there wasn't much to see

a cross on the wall

billowy draped by dead spiderweb

a yellowy portrait of a teenage soldier

stiff jawed and wearing a union army uniform

and on the far side of the room

was a slipshod desk

pushed up against the wall, yes

a stack of books, a lantern

a wine bottle half empty

and a dirty bent stovepipe hat

definitely an old mountain geezer

walter concluded

as he inched toward the desk

head in a carnival spin

once again

he saw the topless maidens

splashing in waves of cash

as he reached out to open one of the drawers

then a sound from the bedroom doorway

a bad sound

a trouble sound

the low growling of an angry dog

cascades of rain sprayed the house with a hiss

and walter truth slowly turned around

hands up

smiling

nice doggy

nice

he lost his breath

when his glassy kaleidoscope eyeballs beheld

there in the doorway — a charnel house vision

not a living dog, no

but the growling animated skeleton of a dog

it leaned forward on bony paws

its phantom construction

creaking in a jerky advance

walter rubbed his eyes

no jesus no

the tiny skeleton started to bark

jaws clacking

ribs shaking and teeth gnashing

walter moved slowly away from the desk

back toward the door

picked up his saddlebag

a house of witchery, he called out

that's what this is!

then from the rear room came a deep voice

shep, stop that barkin' now

what's got into you

is someone here

a visitor

hmmm

a thief?

out of the doorway

walked a tall

lanky

human skeleton

carrying a fiddle

and wearing a tuxedo coat with tails

walter froze, jaw open, drooling

the skeleton made long bowlegged

strides over to the desk

picked up the stovepipe hat

and twisted it on the dirty whiteness of his skull

good evening, sir

mighty bad storm we're havin'

looks like you're all wet

come, sit by the fire

unless you're fixin' to catch a cold

walter couldn't move

terrified, speechless, sure of death

the skeleton laughed

oh, don't let shep bother ya

he gets riled easy

say, what's in that saddlebag

are you a salesman, sir

walter truth managed to nod

sweat like melting ice

pouring off the flush of his temples

the skeleton picked a stringy bow off the desk

and ran it across his fiddle

making a catfight screechy sound

walter felt his pant leg dampen with hot piss

welcome to the house of bones, mr. salesman

you can call me

mr. bones

i am the most notable hobgoblin in these hills

you must've heard of me

of course you've heard of me

why else would you brave

such unpleasant weather

to visit my humble abode

the ghastly apparition laughed

his jaw went clickety clack

sir, may i see what you have for sale

mr. bones, moving

in dips and bobs

like a marionette

put his fiddle and bow down

walked over to walter

picked up the rain-soaked saddlebag and shook
it

what have we here

bottles, hmmm

the skeleton dog had wandered over

and was sniffing walter's shoes

the piss puddle there

mr. bones rifled the bag with his dry skinless
arm

coming up with the blue bottle first

he held it up in the sparkle of firelight

restore skin, restore youth

he read out loud

ah, just what i've been looking for

with hard ivory fingertips he uncapped it

dumping the blue liquid over his shoulders and
ribcage

then he tossed the empty bottle away to smash

and looked down

hoping to see

a miraculous restoration

of his once strapping physique

smiling a lipless grin

waiting

waiting

expectant and waiting

the skeleton tapped his long brittle feet
impatiently

well, how long does it usually take

walter shrugged, still unable to speak

bones shrugged as well

and reached into the saddlebag once again

finding another bottle

this time the one that read

restore muscle, grow muscle

bones clapped skeleton hands together, excited

yes, muscles

oh how i miss my muscles

i used to be a real cock 'o the walk

a pugilist

oh, to have muscles again

yes, yes, yes

once again he poured

the entire contents over his bones

threw the empty bottle away to break

and waited

and waited

mr. bones was visibly upset with the results

he was still all bones

no muscle

no skin

no anything

so that's the kinda traveling salesman you are,
huh

a low life yellow-bellied scum-suckin' con artist

i don't think i like you, sir

i think you're a cheat

and your products are swill

hogwash

if you promise skin and muscle

then you better deliver, you hear

i think it's only right

that you give me your own flesh now

the skeleton turned to his phantom dog

doesn't that seem appropriate, shep

the dog barked agreement

and mr. bones wheeled back off to the desk

sliding open the middle drawer

and coming up with a cleaver

this should do the trick, he cackled

slicing the tarnished blade

with quick swishes through the air

now hold still

the skeleton grimly instructed

and please remove your derby

walter truth's lips pulled away

in a grimace from his discolored teeth

and his derby flew off

as he hopped like a rabbit

right out of his shoes

sorry, but i gotta go, he stammered

then turned away fast

breaking down the door

as easy as a man twice his size

the skeleton dog clamped its jaws

on walter's pant leg

as he frantically untied

his confused wide-eyed horse

the nag, coming to the defense of his owner

gave a hind leg spring action kick to the death
dog

scattering bones in a white explosion

mr. bones was appalled

hinge jaw falling open

as he stepped outside

try to steal from me

and cheat me

and then kick my dog, too

you lousy no good . . .

he swung the cleaver but the clip clop duo were
off

the angry skeleton chasing them into the rain

shiny sharp weapon held high

and glowing by lightning strike

down the road walter and his horse got away

and walter truth didn't know it at that point

but his hair had gone suddenly

and completely white

as he rode off like ichabod into the swirling dark
weather

never thinking twice about turning back

to retrieve his saddlebag

or his precious derby

the door creak

his landlord's wife showed up in her green dress

that was her favorite

it had been her favorite since 1965

but it didn't really fit anymore

it cupped her big curves and made her slither

constant redheaded movement

pressing the tightness down with her freckled
hands

every little twitch purred a grin of flesh and
fabric

she clicked up the sidewalk in her heels

and watched him like a water moccasin

as he struggled off the porch

with another splashing bucket

the damn leaky roof had let another wash of

sadness in

forcing him to mop and scoop

but it never seemed to end

november had been one big downpour

he was dumping his rooms out every few hours

and the landlord's wife liked to interrupt his
work

she'd watch him for a while

without saying anything

popping little red pills

each swallow followed

by three clicks of the red pumps

he tried to ignore her and battle the sadness

chasing the shadows out like bats with a broom

kicking through the front yard leaf piles

and glowering

his neighbors think he's nuts

but the landlord's wife

she thinks he's funny

and cute

the way he struggles with that endless task

the way he struggles to keep things in order

after he'd emptied another bucket into the street

she took a long time waddling over to him

then gave him a long look from head to toe

slowing down around the belt to smile

listen lady, he tells her, your husband

has gotta get on the ball

this house is infested

the rats used to just show up once a week

to play poker and smoke their little cigars

but now they're here three times a day

breakfast, lunch and dinner

and they shit like crazy

i need an exterminator

hell, i need a shrink

she just kept smiling

pressing her green dress down

and sticking her lumpy chest out

baby, why don't you let *me* tell you what you
need?

she walked past him

up on the porch

and through the door

the rats scattered beneath the air raid of her
perfume

and he followed, tossing his bucket in the weeds

shaking his head

and undoing his belt

once by the ocean

the ocean here sings

the same old tune it always has

but it sure sounds different

with the storefronts now stripped

of their big summery blush

drawing back to dirty browns

and the crisp low light

finds every little building boarded up

steel accordion shutters

cracked glass

noises from inside

maybe animals or nosey kids

either way

it's not the folks who owned those places

they're long gone

and the old structures they left behind

suffer the vandalism of weather

while weathering the humiliation of vandals

the boardwalk and boulevard

both a goddamn mess

right over there was the old burlesque den

but there's no burlesque there anymore

just roaches prowling the dirty floor

just the twisting blue shimmy hips

of dancing ghost girls inside

who can collect motes of dust

and make those motes glow

in the tantalizing shapes

of their old bodies

they must sense me

peering through the window boards

because those ghost girls gather up diaphanous
boas

and crawl a ladder of smoke rings into the
ceiling

taking their blue light

back to its rightful owner

the moon

this is a haunted place now

used to be a big tourist attraction

bringing in people from inland frying pan towns

who wanted a face full of salty air

wanted to laugh at the pelicans

tell shark stories

mix drinks at beachside hotels

sand in the lobby and bikini girls rushing by

all once by the ocean here

but not now

the old wooden coaster

has its rusty cars rotting

off and below the black vertebrae

of tracks in waist-high weeds

the scraggly beards

of spanish moss in the moonlight

luminescent and swaying

down from the leaning rails

i watched the wind one day

conjure a rattling ghost car

push it up the first hill

chink chink chink

then drop it whoosh to vanish

in a scatter of dry leaves

ethereal shouts and screams

some long gone

july

the thrill rides are all closed down

without lights or motion

or bodies to toss around

they just sit there

all overgrown and done with

like a salvage yard

like a cemetery

especially now

with the humidity and insect clouds

of high summer gone

a clean and brand-new chill

has returned to the coast

it follows me as i duck

in and out of the buildings

a thirsty graverobber

seeking a swallow of bleakness

to level me through sunnier times

a weight to keep me from floating away

a coffin-shaped anchor

this sad-assed midway does the trick

at least for the time being

because there's no denying

one more big hurricane

could carry it all away for good

clear the slate right back to the basics

right back to the beach

now that would be something

though it makes me wonder

where all the ghosts would go

would the burlesque spirits be too confused

with the lack of a stage

to continue their postmortem striptease

well, if you ask me

once the waves roar back

to carve the shoreline to the ocean's advantage

even the dead will be washed off

because no ghost lives forever

they leave

slow and steady

and more and more

it's already happening

by moonlight

when the seagulls look like vultures

little town called tribulation

it was moments before sunset

the frosty blue decline of the day

in the alley by the liquor store

in the last tinsel-covered month of the year

when a young man in black attire

tumbled from some warm interior

arms full of bottled spirits in bags

on his way to a leathery evening

a practiced and apathetic frown

was an outward indication of his allegiance

to the cultivated brooding of the morbid set

and in his self-absorption

he nearly fell right over the ragged drunk

who was bunched up against the bricks

like a dirty sack of thrown potatoes

a graybeard drunk

glittering eye and all

who suddenly came to life

the contact thrumming him like electricity

wait, he told the young goth

skinny hand raised

wait

if you are on your way to a funeral

there is no need to rush

the dead are blessed with nothing if not patience

linger here a while and let me tell you a story

all i require is a taste of

well

whichever bottle you choose to share

when you hear of the horrors i've witnessed

your own imagined troubles will seem trifles

and every star you see in tonight's sky

will be counted as lucky indeed

the young goth pouted, annoyed

listen, the old drunk said

you'll never hear a tale like mine again

just linger a while with ears open

have mercy on an old fool

don't be an asshole

for whatever reason

the youngster remained in place

his face bored and serene

wisps of black hair fluttering in the chill breeze

but without a word he reached into one of the
bags

removed a pint of popov

and handed it down

speaking only four words

this better be good

the old man uncapped the bottle

cleared his throat and began

once there was a town

far from this land of frozen lakes

down in the green belly of the south

where snakes crawl around the calendar

a smaller town

built on a rumpled rise of land

whose shape was determined

by both the murky water of the surrounding swamps

and the coppery languid flow of a slow river

the town was named after the river

and the river was called tribulation

a fitting name bequeathed by the founder

whose wife and three young girls

died of malaria within a year of their arrival

but instead of fleeing the cradle of his sorrows

with the grim and stubborn determination

characteristic of zealots

who live within the bounds of the old testament

he decided to pass the remainder of his days

in the dreary company

of the tragically departed

rolling up his sleeves

so the swarming mosquitoes

could binge freely the red from his veins

others settled around him and watched

as he went from gray to ashes

the merciful lord he prayed to

finally ended his grief

the day he turned ninety-one

the town he left behind

lasted over two hundred years

not very long really

i was there when it all finally ended

and part of me remains

wandering its empty streets

i can close my eyes

and see it now

a ghost town

what was the final indignity, you wonder?

what prompted all human life to finally flee for good?

this penultimate drag

began nineteen summers ago

with a preacher

preacher cornwall

now, as a man he was far from ordinary

this was a man of visions

a man of supernatural sight

a man who spoke in tongues

a man who spoke to angels

until darker forces

invaded his wavelength

and stripped him of reason

it was a restless midnight that found him strolling

past the church and under the tall pine

into a clearing that leads to the river

a heavy presence in the air above

following him

a heavy presence that cleared the air of insects

and spread like crude oil in still water

the stars vanished along the rim of its expansion

evil was gathering

the preacher looked up

he could hear it humming

like a huge hive of electric bees

moments later something landed

with a rotating hiss of blown grass

some sulfurous presence

some unnamable wickedness

scorched his eyes to near blindness

caused his hair to fall out

the next day he raged about town

gesticulating with fists clenched

all up and down main street he went

carving

with broken glass

stigmata blossoms on his palms

hailing the rapture

the devil arrived in town last night, he bellowed

that king of the fallen angels

has fallen on us now

and his intent is to clear this land for the snakes

flee before he lays a claw on you!

after several hours of this wailing

he was handcuffed

and silenced in a windowless cell

of the county jail

poor preacher cornwall

who would've known

that behind his ravings was an awful truth

several days later he calmed down

was released and consequently treated

to the condescending pity

that only the benighted suffer

but in the weeks that followed

it was apparent that a plague of sorts was
underway

there were some big changes in our little town

no one could shake a sense of unease

folks were irritable and stopped socializing

they stopped mowing their lawns

stopped caring about the softball league

stopped going to church

the preacher himself

turned up dead one day

with a bubblegum machine for a stomach

filled with a pharmacy of bright pills

mouth wide open

lying on the library lawn

flies buzzing

roaches moving in softer places

shortly thereafter

the mayor took to fishing off the bridge

with an un-baited hook and a carton of cigarettes

refusing a response to even the most mundane queries

it wasn't long before he hung himself there

leaving an unorganized tackle box and no note

twirling and creaking above the moving water

no one bothered to cut him down

and in the heavy rain

you might think

he was trying to dance

there was no talk of selecting a new mayor

what was the point

around the same time the police force of tribulation

stopped shaving and took to drinking

heavily and while on duty

the teenagers, as a result, had ample opportunity

to stake their claim as rulers of the new anarchy

but instead turned reflective

withdrawn

even more disagreeable

some of them started writing poetry

which they discussed moodily in the same riverside park

there they drained bottles

and moped

and sometimes fought

but never did they laugh or dream or plan

old kicks and pleasures had lost their luster

you could walk down main street to the river

and on the sidewalk you'd see the trash

the heart-rending trash

of torn-up love letters

all hopeless and unleashed to face the elements

blown like desiccated birds with broken wings

up against the buildings

the downtown dark and empty

the barber shop chairs draped

in dusty white sheets

mice darting zig zags

across unswept hair clippings

all because one day the barber got the blues so
bad

he couldn't bear to hold his scissors

he no longer saw the need to look presentable

so downcast, despondent, and sorry

the citizens of tribulation

with bags born of worry beneath their eyes

started to wander around at sundown

aimlessly in clothes they'd been wearing for days

one of these morbid wanderers was little mary
marx

a quiet girl to begin with

she stopped talking completely one day

taking to somnambulism

you could find her at any hour

wandering the streets

a tiny wraith in her flowing pajamas

clutching a pillow to her breast

face all drained to mantle grey

long blonde hair once combed and lovely

now a nest for sparrows

she would shuffle along the narrow walks

searching the ground

as if looking for a decent place

to set down her pillow and sleep

but there weren't many decent places left

not in tribulation

so she took that pillow and that insomnia to the
river

begged for a bed on the black waters

the water obliged

a peaceful bubbling compliance

slipping all cool and clean

into lungs so pink and fair

her heart a bloody island

that no longer labored

she went floating an ophelia ballet

downstream into the rainswell

where alligators waited

while those teenagers smoked

and watched

despondent on the wooden park rail

one of them whistling a half-hearted taps

as little mary marx

chased by rejuvenated fishes

drained of spirit

went spinning out of sight

she was not alone

the old local bluesman, for instance

once a smiling good-natured citizen

but no longer

he started referring to himself as johnny casket

and formed a trio

collectively called the deep sleepers

armed with a bunch of new tunes

they played nightly in the park

without permits or warning

new tunes like 'baby, i feel like shit today'

and 'don't go kill yourself, woman, before you
kill me'

joey krapp played the drums

samuel kilgore played bass

those boys rarely made it through a whole song

without collapsing into arguments

or convulsive fits of terrible weeping

they wore matching suits

with nooses instead of neckties

and the best of their songs

were about crows

inspired by the swelling murder of these birds

who had taken up residence

in the downtown trees

a flapping ever-present cawing pestilence

and when a gun would go off

from some new suicide somewhere

they would lift to complain in great inky storm-
clouds

deafening in their anger, those crows

circling and wheeling until finally

they would calm down to resume

their gloomy perches

never did i see any large bat-winged demons

with widows-peaks and pitchforks

hovering like gargantuan wasps against a

nuclear red sky

although certainly this would've been evidence

that stronger diabolical forces were at work

it was only the crows

and the clouds

and the rain

and a low murmur of sobs

that went on unabated through the night

once happy bedrooms where couples frolicked

were now darkened by the ugly compromises

of sex without pleasure

it was all boring and pointless

and torturous and humid as hell

those left were resigned

to wait with laconic patience for death

in the forgiving company of fellow casualties

turning to ashes like our long-suffering town
founder

whose ghost was seen more and more often

dragging four skeletons

manacled in the rusty jewelry of long chains

up and down the streets

streets buckled and sprouting weeds

the grey-bearded drunk stopped

took a long pull on the vodka

it was safe again

the young man in black had walked off yawning

halfway through his crazy bullshit

the undertow of the yuletide

a cold december night

sleigh bells in the distance

the last of the fireplace embers throbbing orange

fading so fast we should probably close the flue

and we should also unplug the lights

make sure all the doors are locked

so no maniac comes in and steals all those
presents

but all of that can wait a few minutes

because i see that we have

a sleepy person in need of a fable

well, let's see

i can tell you about a cat

who used to live in the city

yes, i certainly could

here is the image

mack the tabby cat

gaunt with hunger bellyaches

and stroking the brittle of his whiskers

was over on the west avenue bridge

in a desperately sad mood

as the midnight hour rolled in

it was cold

six below zero

and he was blinking feline eyes

drowsy feline eyes

watery, blurred

making it hard to focus

making it hard to see

but the bleak festive of the sparkling skyline

engaged his curiosity and drew his gaze

into the faraway tall buildings

where here and there in the hazy distance

some red lights could be found

festooned and flashing

along with evergreen shapes of triangular green

sporadic holiday outbursts

sad old-fashioned attempts

to beat back the darkness

the solstice

the waning

the dwindling hours of another year

it was christmas eve

in the big gray city

it was always

the saddest day on the calendar for mack

it reliably compelled him to reflect on past
yuletides

and no amount of catnip

could steer his remembrances

down other thoroughfares

he had tried

getting high just made it worse

so he was facing the northerly wind

stone cold sober

the northerly wind

that swept off the river

to ruffle the matted finery of his fur

and with a quivering arch of his nimble spine

he paced

back and forth on the edge of that frozen bridge

paws collecting ice with every four-legged stride

he peeked over and down

lambent jags drifting in the black water below

a lone gray seagull hovering mysteriously

near the surface

presumably lost and estranged

like every creature trapped outside

at this hour

on this night

he wished he had been lucky enough

to become a bar cat

it had happened to his old

scrounge-around friend louis

some human bartender started feeding him

in an alley

at first dog biscuits but then beef

and bits of salmon

eventually the brawny gentlemen lured louis
inside

and when the door shut behind him

he was gone for good

never to set paws on pavement again

that's how louis became the celebrated mascot

of the blackfish bar on terrace avenue

the bloated regulars spoiled that lucky cat

to fluffy pillow size

soon his fur always smelled like smoke

and he waddled with a wheeze

but it was a mollycoddle life

full of warmth and plenty

and good old louis was happy

he came to mind because

it had been a year ago

christmas eve

that mack saw him last

mack had been with some other viper cats

sharing catnip behind a dumpster

and then went meandering all frisky

through the fresh twinkling nightfall

somehow he found himself

dodging trouser legs on terrace avenue

and there was the blackfish bar

and there was big round louis

staring out

from beneath a bar window holly wreath

the two exchanged knowing glances

sad meows

heartbreaking

the rest of the night was spent in a blue spiral

and mack had successfully avoided that block
ever since

seeing louis getting more rotund and more
content

for a while was a good thing

but last christmas it had been too much

not every cat gets taken in

not by a long shot

and those that do are wise to count their
blessings

some city cats recommended

that mack take his chances at a shelter

but for him it seemed a death sentence

his life had started there

and nearly ended there on another christmas eve

the first he had a memory of

there was smoke

at about three in the morning

tiny nose pressed through the grill of his cage

sniffing at the first tendrils

he remembered fellow cats

pacing and mewling

he remembered

the terrible chorus of barking dogs

thundering the walls

and then the rising heat

the rising flames

the rising panic

the axe crashing of wood

and the breaking of glass

two firefighters wearing masks tromping
through

opening every cage they could

there was a momentary fumbling of the keys

a quick jostling of the lock

then the cage door was yanked open

mack took flight

through hellish sprays of water

glowing thunderheads of smoke

and into homelessness

he had been making it on his own ever since

and returning to the shelter

after all these years

just wasn't an option

besides, he was just too old and scarred up now

he was just

too old

the wind vibrated the bridge cables to hum

the girders groaned

it was a long way down

mack the tabby cat sneezed

another christmas eve

in the same old city

funny

he never did know his birthplace

but he always claimed christmas eve

as his birthday

and he always imagined

that he had some farm cat in him

yes, he imagined that he was born somewhere

out in the frosty boondocks

sequestered safely in a squirming litter of
muddy calico

in the darkened sanctuary of a hayloft

in the middle of a snowstorm

some old red barn with a black rooster
weathervane

pitchforks on wall pegs

the quiet thresher and the cobwebbed sickle

the shadowy hulk of a slumbering tractor

the high whistling of the wind

through the december fields

mack added these details to his personal
mythology

and every cat who knew him

knew the story

he had been born to swipe claws

at leaping field mice

and meow treats from the farmer's wife

born to swat at the tiny flies

in the pumpkin vines

and rub against old rocking chairs

on a big wraparound porch

some forested land nearby to explore and hunt

a big open sky

a big open moon

to hush the night and coax shy stars out to play

shy stars that never shone

through the city murk and glare

mack loved talking about those country skies

as they existed in his mind

not tethered by actual recollections

this was the invented origin he settled on

he said he ended up a kitten in the city shelter

because the farmer's wife withered into the
grave

and her city relatives did the rest

mack used this tale to help explain

why he felt so out of place

mired in all that concrete

and why he always felt drawn to

abandoned lots and warehouse fields

those oh so precious vacuums of urban neglect

where the tall weeds and briars of the natural
landscape

had been allowed to resume and spread

overgrowth and old trees were what he always
looked for

even though these places

were predictably diminished

by discarded trash and bum shelters and such

mack liked to use his imagination

when he stalked there

treading lightly on the broken glass

and rusted mufflers

picturing those fabricated hayseed evenings

in his mind

transforming every city mouse he saw

into one of those long-tailed field mice

of the boondocks

imagining stars above

imagining a place

where he belonged

goddamn christmas eve

it started to snow lightly

flakes of white floating down post haste

floating down post haste

from the thick and blackened yarnings

of the bruised and sable snow-clouds

gathering in new glittering clumps

on every manhole cover and curbside car

mack heard the sound of dogs barking
somewhere

canine belligerent and frantic they echoed

sounded like ghost dogs

our tabby cat shivered

he was feeling the undertow

a rapid frozen current

filled with corkscrews of tinsel

castaway candy canes

discarded mistletoe

seasonal drownings

the cruel sinking and choking sensation

which is only fully understood

by the disenfranchised and lost

that old gasping for air that occurs

on every family holiday

for those without any real sort of family to speak
of

mack the tabby cat could be counted in these
ranks

and he would be the first

warm-blooded creature to confirm

that the wicked undertow of the yuletide

administers a potent dose of loathing

that marks the lonely for life

all wayfaring outsiders with functioning hearts

typically possess these interior alterations

as well as their resulting sympathies

it binds them in brotherhood

and sisterhood

and for what

he wondered

christmas fucking eve

mack paced the steel balustrade

of that west avenue bridge

and he looked down into that gliding ice

those grim wave undulations

he stopped his ritual padding

and leaned back on his haunches

in pounce position

the time has come for me

why not in the last hour

of my ninth year

nine years in survival mode

is a good run

my time here is used up

there are other places to be

he meowed

all that remains

is a further disintegration

of my physical frame

the increased brittle collapse

of an already shaky skeleton

an unstoppable weakening

not sustainable in survival mode

nine years in survival mode

lots of wear and tear

the dulling of the senses

the decline of dexterity and pounce

probably kidney issues

and those roving packs of burly stray dogs

they will eventually catch me

the worst ending for a cat

death by a flurry of bloody canine chompings

much better to leap into the unknown

courageous and compliant

than to perish

due to weakness

he paused

another snowy gust shook him backwards

and took his sense of smell quite suddenly by
surprise

because in that frozen river wind he found

an old familiar scent

one that he had never fully forgotten

the pissy and perfumed smell

of a persian lady cat he briefly knew

one who still stubbornly resided all reclined and
lovely

in each thumping red ventricle of his heart

and on every glowing stage

in the dream-box of his mind

her name was nancy

he knew her for two weeks in december

a snow-white longhair

who got left behind in the bustle

by some millionaire lush trophy wife

drifting through her holiday travels

mack would've been better off

had he never found her at all

but she was lucky he came along

she would've been knocked up or dead

by the end of that very night

if not for him

mack smiled sadly to himself

he closed his eyes and could still see her

confused and cowering

mewling by that fire hydrant

she was not prepared for life on the outside

she was tiptoeing pathetically in the slush

he knew he had to take care of her

so in the days that followed

he looked after her

and quite predictably

and quite disastrously

he fell in love

ridiculous

what a sap

love makes all sentient creatures

act dangerously against instinct

and in this pathetic state he made sure she didn't
starve

he guarded her from the excitable neighborhood
libertines

and the whole brief time

he should've known better

the street can't keep cats that lovely for very long

it was only a matter of days before she returned

to a life of milk dishes and steady meals

like louis

nancy was gone for good

never to set paws on pavement again

some thin-waisted human dancer

who lived near the city university

had caught a glimpse of my persian obsession

and snatched her up

everything happens so fast in the life of a cat

mack looked down into the river again

there was a large red ball floating

it was visible for a moment

then some unseen force sucked it under

he took a deep breath

sneezed

then launched himself

into the whistling air

flipping over once

the bridge railing receding

upwards and away

he was stunned

that he had actually done it

after such a long time pacing

there he was

legs instinctively spread like wings

sailing and spinning toward his death

flashes of light fired in his eyes

like brilliant screaming fireworks

and then his cat body crashed

with a splintering fatal crack

onto a sheet of river ice

those screaming fireworks were silenced

and in their place

came a soundless line

of fuzzy bouncing red shapes

bringing warmth

floating warmth

each of these shapes expanded

then dimmed to darker hues as they collided

forming one seamless purple firmament

which began twinkling with stars

a clear winter night sky

a clear winter

country sky

mack realized he had paws

and he produced claws to playfully swipe

and then he was pouncing through frozen corn
fields

toward a barn draped in strings of red lights

there was a festive glowing

coming from within

shafts of light spread out

like parallel strands of glowing ribbon

unfurled and continuing to unfurl

lovely

incomprehensibly lovely

these ribbons began moving

tugged by playful owners

begging for pounces

and he reared back on his haunches

head darting back and forth

tracking those ribbons

as they were pulled gently

away

migration and captivity in low light

sleeping with a wet rag

on my hot face

sick on the old couch

curtains open wide

to the snowstorm

waking up every few minutes

to watch the wind

throw sheets of white

against the glass

and my cat

who was crouched in the darkness

would look back at me

sometimes

when i coughed

with snow dervishes

and bones rattling the vents

curtains open wide

to the storm

about the author

Bob Stevens is a former party store manager, current librarian, and native Michigander. This is his third book in a planned collection of thirteen.

jrefund books (the first eight)

01 dark tales of the inland seas region (2019)

02 dark poems of the inland seas region (2020)

03 dark poems of elsewhere (2021)

04 dark tales of elsewhere (2022)

05 devil in the pines (2023)

06 the last island almanac (2024)

07 the last academic library (2025)

08 the last inland seas unraveling (2026)